WHISPERS OF DYING LEAVES

Arvind Kapoor

ZORBA BOOKS

ZORBA BOOKS

Published by Zorba Books, December 2025
Website: www.zorbabooks.com
Email: info@zorbabooks.com
Author Name: Arvind Kapoor

Title: Whispers of Dying Leaves

Printbook ISBN: 978-93-5896-037-2
Ebook ISBN: 978-93-5896-649-7

Zorba Books Pvt. Ltd. (opc)
Sushant Arcade,
Next to Courtyard Marriot,
Sushant Lok 1, Gurgaon – 122009, India

Printed in India

Dedication

To my sons, Siddharth and Kartikeya, whose childhoods blossomed like flowers in the spring sun and who now stand tall as trees touched by the sky. You have been the rivers that led me to the heart of nature, the winds that carried me toward unknown horizons. In your laughter, the forest found its song; in your wonder, I found my roots and wings alike. This collection blooms from the seeds of our shared journeys—echoes of love, growth, and the endless landscapes of the soul.

Contents

Foreword to "Whispers of Dying Leaves"

This poetry collection invites readers on an intimate voyage through the landscapes of human experience—shadows of suffering, the delicate whispers of memory, the awakening of spirit, and the eternal presence of nature's witness.

Each poem is a fragment of a larger meditation on survival and solitude, on longing and release, on the quiet turns of transformation under the vast sky. The poems traverse the raw terrain of pain and resilience, silently pulse with the music of inner reflection, and ultimately rise to embrace the luminous thresholds of hope and renewal. They remind us that beneath our stories of fracture and loss lie enduring connections—to ourselves, to one another, and to the natural world's ceaseless cycle of death and rebirth. As you move through the chapters, you encounter voices both fragile and fierce, shadows receding before the dawning light, and a persistent flame of healing. This collection celebrates poetry's ability to hold and transform suffering, to listen deeply, and to reveal the profound beauty hidden even in silence and shadow.

May these poems offer solace, inspire courage, and awaken your own sense of wonder and renewal. This title and foreword reflect the collection's core themes, emotional depth, and the transformative journey presented by the poems, inviting readers into a meaningful engagement with the text.

Foreword to haiku: soliloquy of seasons

Lyrical journeys through nature's seasons mirror the ebb and flow of human emotion. Moments of tranquility and transience weave through imagery of wind, water and light. Time passes quietly, leaving reflections and memories in the wake.

Foreword to tanka: on the sands of time

Every poem in this collection drifts like a wave—rising from quiet reflection, cresting with emotion, and retreating into soft silence. These verses trace the rhythm of the heart as it converses with the river, the sea, and the sky. At times tranquil, at times restless, they explore the tides of longing, memory, and rediscovery. Each piece stands alone yet connects subtly to the next, like ripples born from the same drop of moonlight. Across shifting nights, forgotten shores, and familiar winds, the poems evoke fragments of love, transience, and solace found in nature's eternal cycle. In these verses, the world pauses between dusk and dawn, where solitude becomes a companion and the horizon whispers back to those who listen.

CHAPTER 1

Shadows and Suffering

1. Claws and Shadows

Fox cub, hind legs shattered
by a sadist's shot.
Its journey home becomes
a crawl through travail and suffering,
hiding from death's jeers,
from the buzzing swarm—
ants, flies, a chameleon
clinging to its wounds.

Each mile stretches thin,
time swollen with pain.
The vixen gathers strength alone,
while siblings chase softer prey,
their play sharpening skills
on easier targets.

Survival now means solitude—
half-days of hiding,
snatched naps with a third eye open,
warding off jaws, talons,
or the curious paw of an adventurer.

Does the cub learn the craft—
to kill, to vanish, to endure?
Yes, but promise is fragile,
threaded with anxiety,
for there is no real home:
only a helpless mother,
attacks that never sleep,
a future clouded and dim.

So it is with the defiled tween,
child of a widowed mother,
hand gripping the railing,
the other raised to fend.
Unlike siblings, he carries friends—
their faith like quiet armor.
He grows strong where scars are deep,
forgiving,
unburdened by hangovers of hate.

***

2. Night's Hostage

it's only at bedtime
that buried thoughts rise—
playing jingles in singles,
gathering like storms
to carry away sleep
to forsaken shores,
still holding me hostage.

shadows weave in silence,
tracing the walls with cold fingers,
whispering secrets
that were never meant to be heard.

lost? they never were.
no sleep tonight.

***

3. Erosion

This is different—
Not the sudden flood,
nor the swollen banks of a river,
not the thunder of waves
shattering a shore.

This is different—
Not wildfire consuming a forest,
nor the glow of a funeral pyre,
not the silence after
a kingdom has burned.

This is different—
Not the vast Sahara,
nor a hollowed stone,
not dust upon dust,
not bone upon bone.

This is different—
Not the grip of nightmares,
nor the pit without end,
not the black of unspoken sins,
nor the starless absence of light.

This is the erosion of the unseen,
where beliefs soften and collapse,
where values sour in silence,
where debates drift without reasons,
and meals are cooked without taste.

It is the slow unmaking—
not of land, nor fire, nor bone,
but of meaning itself.

***

4. Fragile Dreams

We squabbled and babbled
over pebbles and rubble,
while being swindled,
while being squandered—
our appeals to idealism
hollowed, rendered meaningless.

Yet still, people clung
desperately, hopelessly,
to impossible dreams.

And in the quiet aftermath,
we watched shadows of hope
flutter like tattered flags,
grasping for meaning
where none had yet taken root.

***

5. Untied & Untimely

my fragile mind
counts a million seconds
to untie and retie
lifelong knots —
a thousand pieces of you
gathered from the unlikely places
where you shed them, unknowing,
stitching them into an accidental collage.

you, in a breathless flicker,
measure hundreds of years of us
in a few indifferent milliseconds —
our clocks misread, out of stride,
and leave the work of a lifetime
dangling between your hurry and my slow hands.

— small hands, patient as ruins,
trying to make a portrait from scattered weather.

***

6. Tremors of Her Nearness

I taste it with my eyes—
the lingering warmth of her skin,
her fragrance circling like a spell,
while storms of longing rise
in the darkening horizon of her gaze.

Her nearness hums like silk on air,
a murmur against the quiet,
soft as twilight fingers
tracing the edges of my breath.

My fragile embankments tremble,
muddy bunds threatened
by the swelling flood of her turbulence—

a waiting ecstasy,
ticking,
ready to explode.

***

7. Burden Beneath The Saddle

The horse walks on,
thoughtless, steady,
hooves meeting earth
as though the path were endless.

The stirrup's feather-touch
reminds the jockey
not of power,
but of the weight she must carry again—
not the beast beneath her,
but the invisible yoke
of hunger, discipline, and demand.

Her stomach hollow,
her body honed into lightness,
she becomes a vessel of will—
a mind astride flesh,
riding a creature
that mirrors her obedience.

The horse submits to reins,
she submits to rules;
each bound by silence,
each compelled by expectation.

And so,
in the quiet rhythm of hoofbeats,
lingers the question:
is it the beast that carries the rider,
or the rider who carries
the heavier burden?

***

8. The Hand That Isn't Mine

Is this my place—
crowds of shadows
telling old stories,
suffering as if it were prayer.

A smile,
a hand reaching—
sinewed, spotted,
not mine.
The glass slips;
water runs away.

Fewer faces now.
Friends gone—
yet their laughter
echoes down the corridor,
schoolbags colliding with baby cries,
festivals with firelight,
beaches with hills.

A woman drifts beside me,
changing shape,
her voice unpinned.
She lies on the floor—
unmoving.
I watch through a wall,
unable to touch.

A stranger explains death
like a school lesson.
The tired close their eyes.

I look out—
no stars, no moon.
Perhaps they rest
in my mother's lap,
where kisses
once smothered me in song.

The tune returns.
My eyelids sink.
At the gate—
a man with a bicycle,
sacks across his shoulder.
He smiles,
tired,
familiar.

***

9. Ashes of Silence

The smoke ascended,
not merely from timber,
but from centuries of muted cries.

Flames—zealous acolytes—
devoured the fragile walls of captivity,
until the hut of submission collapsed
into a humbled heap of embers.

From the wound of charred wood
she stepped forth,
a woman once gagged by silence,
her eyes burning brighter than the ruins,
her breath heavy with ash—
yet laced with the fragrance
of long-delayed freedom.

For in the collapse of prisons,
the soul does not perish—
it rises, unshackled,
to inhale eternity.

***

CHAPTER 2

Silence, Memory, and Longing

1. Unfathomable She

Unfathomable she —
does she look at you,
or past you, through you,
reading the absence you carry?

Perhaps it is her shadow she studies,
the one that melted into night
or was erased by light —
a silent companion
she has yet to reclaim.

Has she tuned inward, listening,
to secret music or to waves
that strike her hidden core,
or to an inner volcano
dampened by patient hands
unknown to her fellow travelers?

Yet there is a glow in her stillness,
a pulse that waits beneath restraint —
not the silence of defeat
but the gathering of dawn,
not a wound concealed
but a seed preparing to break open.

She walks the path
with eyes both distant and near,
holding a truth no shadow can smother,
a quiet flame that grows
as if the stars themselves
had chosen her heart
for their dwelling place.

***

2. Meditative Reflection

In the still water of a pond,
bubbles rise at random—
like forgotten voices
seeking air.

Are they fragments of memory,
drifting upward
from the depths of silence?
Are they longings,
once buried,
now daring to speak?

The pond reminds me—
what is hidden
never rests forever;
even in silence,
the soul finds a way
to breathe.

***

3. Incantation of Silence

Waves sleep,
froth whispers.

The sun descends
the western stair.

Birds do not return,
nests breathe emptiness.

The wind waits
behind the mountains.

Leaves clutch the earth,
till the lone star rises.

Silence reigns.
Only poets stir—
restless keepers of shadows,
weaving night
into eternity.

***

4. Setting Sun

A setting sun, and I—half-submerged,
as waves rise to caress my face,
softly erasing freckles of the day.

In awe, I watch the sky dissolve:
yellow and orange surrender
to the quiet dusk of bluish-brown.

Beneath me, the waves conspire,
removing sand grain by grain,
a gentle theft of certainty.

Then the moon ascends, serene,
a silver reminder that dreams
still want me alive.

Reluctantly, I rise,
carrying both the sea's embrace
and the ache of leaving.

***

5. Moonlight Memories

Glide on fickle waves,
Slide along rugged trunks,
Ousted from leaves by wandering wind.

Nothing lets it pause—
Except on paths to courtyards and fields,
Where dreams wield their quiet magic,
Or when alone, I yield to it.

It lingers on stone and soil,
Whispers in the hush of night,
A silver trace on shadowed eyes,
A fleeting touch, then gone.

***

6. Sharing Secrets

Scattered in gusts and swirls—
a cup of forest spice,
filling the hollow of the mundane,
soothing the bruises of daily strife.

Sip the nectar
spilled on flowers and leaves,
steeped in the magic of a fog-laden night,
holding thoughts
with wings of infinite flight.

The moon hums low
through branches veined with light,
while hidden streams compose
a song of silver threads—
a hymn the earth remembers.

***

7. A Sunday Sojourn

Back to my college—
a drifting return,
where stories cross and uncross
like faint echoes,
muffled laughter dissolves
into whispering paths,
erudite gazes blur,
runaway glances vanish,
fragrances linger
like half-remembered songs,
dances dissolve
into the hush of empty corridors.

I reach for them—
but they fade,
haze upon haze,
the times I miss.

***

8. Gate of Reverie

At the gate stood an undecided I,
remembering the unoiled hinges,
her delicate hands resting over them.
The noise followed,
then quick footsteps
stirring a napping world.

The memories still linger there,
mingling with the garden's aroma.

A shadow of time drifts between the bars,
catching fragments of laughter,
and the scent of blooms
that no longer speak,
yet whisper in the quiet air.

***

9. Crossings

Beneath the bridge they waited—
above, a train of thoughts chugged past:
freedom bartered,
battles fought,
moments earned,
events lost.

A hush of wind,
the river listening,
carrying whispers
no one claimed.

At last, moving away
from the native place,
they found the quiet,
the fulfilment sought,
the peace unnamed.

***

10. Just Another Goodbye

Partings erode me,
a shore yielding to time's tide.
Am I only
the sum of fleeting moments?

Not a tree in autumn,
I am a river:
cradling moss, leaves, twigs,
even stones that slip away.

And yet I keep moving,
carrying echoes of laughter,
the whispered weight of memories,
until they dissolve into the current.

***

11. Whispers on the Dew

a silken voice distills
through the thoughtful night—
not on the tap of feet,
but on the heart's silent beat.

it lifts an ecstatic bosom,
entranced by a singing hoodlum.
tell me—how long, do you think,
a leaf can cradle its dew?
is it the weight of feeling,
or the waiting moments, too?

then drifts a hidden lantern,
casting shadows made of light—
dreams dissolve like incense smoke,
rising slowly out of sight.

***

12. Twilight Fantasies

Twilight fantasies gather
beneath the canopy of shadows,
tenderly touching horizons
where old images hide in memory.

With night's arrival
they drift into dreams,
leaving behind longings—
agonies abundant
to greet the morning.

And in the stillness between stars,
a secret choir hums unheard,
spilling silver threads of silence
across the fragile fabric of sleep.

***

13. Echoes Through the Woods

It gave a gurgling gasp
as rain came rushing in,
filling the veins of thirsty streams—
a sound that lingers still,
etched upon the hush of memory.

But winter's breath
has frozen all feeling;
the trees, stripped bare,
stand solemn in witness.
Only the widowed wind remains,
a restless mourner,
whistling its sorrow,
howling its grief
through the haunted woods.

Yet beneath the silence,
a secret stirs unseen—
roots dream of thawing earth,
of waters flowing free,
and the tender promise of spring.

***

14. A Different Set of Eyes

I stand now
with a changed gaze—
the glitter of hurried business
charms me no longer.

What once was mundane
breathes of creation:
the murmur of water
caressing thirsty soil,
a vow of nurture
to the hidden seeds.

The earth exhales its first consent,
a fragrance rising,
petrichor filling the lungs—
a secret language
we share with rain and root.

So much waits
to be entered,
to be felt,
to be surrendered to—
before humanity
calls itself all-knowing.

***

CHAPTER 3

Awakening and Transformation

1. The Pottery

Is poetry a vessel of smooth clay,
turned flawless on the wheel,
meant to be admired at a glance—
or must it bear the thumbprints of the maker,
the ridges where fingers pressed too hard,
the glaze that ran uneven,
a hairline crack that whispers of fire and struggle?

Its worth may lie in what resists perfection:
a rim that pinches the lip,
a curve that jars the eye,
designs that stagger like uneven brushstrokes,
yet shimmer with secret intention.

Such a vessel does not flatter—it unsettles.
It pricks the skin like a shard left unfiled,
snags the hand mid-caress,
breaks the trance of habit,
rouses the sleeper with its sharp edge.

It unsettles peace like a mole on a cheek
that the gaze cannot leave,
like strands of hair tangled in the comb
that refuse to yield.

True poetry reshapes us—
images fracture, scatter,
then gather again in new alignments.

A pot once broken,
fired anew in a different kiln,
its cracks gilded with thought,
becomes the vessel we did not expect
but cannot forget.

***

2. Whispers of the Hidden Realm

In the shadows,
where unseen worlds awaken,
ancient shades guard their secrets,
concealed from the blinding glare of light.

There, truth is not spoken—
it is breathed like incense,
drifting softly toward seekers,
toward those who walk inward paths
with silent reverence.

Compassion, love, and gratitude
move like eternal currents,
unfolding gently,
as if the Divine were spilling nectar
across the soul's horizon.

Contours dissolve into oneness,
yet for eyes attuned,
the sacred design glimmers—
a vision only the awakened can behold.

***

3. The Purity of Effort

As you untangle relations
that have knotted into naught,
the path steepens—
a hill of unseen weight.

You maneuver past boulders,
clutch at slippery vines,
while pebbles disturb
the fragile rhythm of thought.

You recall a tale—
of life breathed back
by tender touch
upon lifeless bones.
But it is never so.

Awakening arrives differently:
not with revival of form,
but as a quiet dawn
of spirit renewed,
a consciousness steeped
in the purity of heart.

And then you know—
Love is not proved by endings,
but revealed in the striving itself.
The essence is not in what survives,
but in the sincerity of effort,
where purity alone abides.

***

4. Horizons High

If you love me,
do not pin me to a vase—
do not smother with an always-hold.
Give me the small latitude of air;
let the wind adore me tenderly.

While I live, take my scent with you,
do not pluck the petals before their hour—
the earth will sing when we return.

If you love me, let me rise
to distant horizons.
Gaze, and keep your questions hidden.
Do not barter me into water;
I am the child's sudden laugh,
a ribbon of smoke and fog—
the restless thought that keeps you awake.

***

5. Between Shadow and Radiance

a breakaway cloud
and an estranged me
adrift in our orbits
like nameless vagabonds
measuring the depths,
the immeasurable vastness of life

in the murmur of waves,
in the chanting winds,
we stumble upon our purpose—
our lives so alike,
yet clothed in different forms

and somewhere between
shadow and radiance,
an unseen hand scatters
seeds of silence,
from which new worlds
whisper themselves awake

***

6. Where Roads Fade

do i need my way lit so profusely
while walking a dusty road to nowhere
with only sparse clouds of banished anxiety
whether the road climbs uphill
or slips into a valley
does it matter

for a restless soul passing through
a changing, challenging world

and yet, even in silence and shadow
the smallest spark of curiosity
traces the edges of possibility
like sunlight on drifting dust

***

CHAPTER 4

Nature's Witness

1. The Sea, the Moon, and the Broken Shore

The whole night, the Sea writhed in spasms,
its banks bearing the ache of repeated assaults.
The Moon, indifferent, laughed at the Sea's arousal,
while the vegetation turned its face in hatred of that pale light.

The whole night, the Sea lost its senses,
poisoned by the silver rays.
Its waves were flung away like orphans,
only to return—tramps seeking shelter they could never own.

The whole night, the storm tormented the trees,
birds prayed for their fragile young in trembling nests.
Lovers of the Sea stood aghast at its cruelty,
while the broken banks wept into the darkness.

And the whole night, the Sky bore its own burden—
feeling the sting of pins that fastened stars to its skin.
Yet it whispered gratitude to fate,
for its suffering was gentler than that of the bleeding shore.

***

2. Ephemeral Echoes

a sudden precipitation
shatters the forest's quiet spell
an abrupt rush over fragile plants
hoisting flowers skyward
leaving colors and scents
traced like whispers on the earth
a bugle of the last post

petrichor rises slowly
to console the wounded souls
and eyes that have forgotten wonder

in the stillness afterward
droplets cling like fleeting thoughts
each one a reminder
that all is transient,
yet everything leaves its mark
on the fragile weave of being

and in this gentle undoing
the forest breathes,
teaching patience, release,
and the quiet grace of impermanence

***

3. In an Emerald Sea

A seasoned seafarer is never lulled
by the emerald calm—
he feels the tremor beneath,
the whispered promise of rising waves.

He knows the sea is willful,
seductive in its glitter,
harboring tempests
that can strip an oarman's craft
to splinters of surrender.

Yet he sails on,
trusting the dialogue of wind and tide,
his heart attuned to danger's music,
for only those who risk the sea's embrace

***

4. Sea of Fantasies

in the Sea of Fantasies
we sail to unknown shores
each holding its own horizon—
an azure of deep serenity,
a secretive thoughtful grey,
a passion-soaked vermillion,
an elation of another chance.

in the colors of a kaleidoscope,
in the vibrating notes of prayer,
we float—perennial, unbound.

and sometimes the wind whispers
tales of unseen lands,
where time bends softly
and the heart learns
the language of stars.

***

5. Tattered Reflections

Weary waves drift into palm shade,
seeking meaning in the sea's ache,
flung from shore to restless shore—
the Sun scatters its million mirrors,
laughing at the broken glimmers.

And a human life feels much the same:
struggles tossed, torn by hands unseen,
yet even his wounds become bright sparks
for others to fasten their sails
on his ragged, floating frame.

But listen closer—beneath the roar,
the sea keeps a secret undertone:
pain and joy are braided strands,
and every shattered fragment gleams
with the possibility of wholeness.

***

6. Whispers of the Dawn

Vanishing dreamy fawns
amid protesting yawns,

Floating in the mantras of a temple,
sliding into silken sheet pleats they resemble.
Somewhere, a hungry dog barks
like fog suddenly blown away.

In queue line up the awaiting schedule,
like a matador's pawing bull.
I wake to life's relentless tugging pulls.

And in the hush before the sun claims the sky,
shadows stretch and yawn,
memories slip like water through fingers,
while the heart listens to its own quiet hymn

***

7. First Stroke

She hid the pencils,
the canvas, the colors—

yet inside her
lay the spark
I sought in empty rooms
and borrowed skies.

In the silence,
my pulse collided with hers,
every touch of smooth silk
igniting something raw,
a feverish thrill
in a man
holding a brush
for the first time.

***

8. Whistling with Hope

Whistling with hope
on the way to her abode,
love-rhymes I unload,
whizzing down a lonely road.

Just before I meet her
my thoughts are slowed,
playing hide-and-seek—
a drifting, vanishing code.

In a galaxy I float,
abandoned in space,
searching for the key
to unlock her grace.

And I wonder if love
is etched in the skies—
a silent equation,
revealed through our eyes.

***

CHAPTER 5

Haiku: Soliloquy of Seasons

the flowers
fall
for a breeze

blossoms cling
to tired branches
as autumn alights

luscious leaves
kiss dewy leaves
an early bright sun

a wandering in time
a lone leaf on a windy wind
a warbler lifts its pitch

in a demure lake
float a pair of birds—
an undercurrent of love

applying balm
to a chaotic day:
calm of a sunset

short
excited waves
vanish on the shore

on an idyllic shoal
the sunsets
console

a spicy sea,
a scented breeze,
a nonchalant moon

chilly nights,
foggy days—
suspended sentences

under the watch
of a weak winter sun
an adamant ice sheet

tender tales
of winter escapades,
early sunsets

heavenly sights,
tranquil delights,
slip by unannounced

lucid moments
in a chugging life—
gathering memories

vivid memories thrive
in moments gone by—
nothing to hold onto

alone on a holiday,
watching waves dissipate
the bygone times

undisturbed
images play in water:
a gallery divine

amid celebrations
karma walks in
silently

torrent of
broken images—
an unmoved sun

endless points
on a rim,
going nowhere

earth trembles,
houses crumble,
hopes gamble

a daily magic:
walking in moonlight
bares the soul

merrily
she played—
away crowds swayed

CHAPTER 6

Tanka Collection: On the Sands of Time

❀

it's just a poetry
with it's twists & turns
an ode to the river
where words evolve
to the beats of the heart

❀

sky with clouds shorn
on a summer morn
a detached bay
and an abandoned me
remember you

❀

a setting Sun &
a tranquil sea
adrift of daily chaos
love stories unfold
with poems in tow

❀

a cosmos and
many a black holes
a bare truth
why so afar
i wonder

❀

i hop
to the bus stop
imagining things
of nocturnal flings
childhood dreams

❀

another
dreamy evening
the calm
cannily cultures
for the lovers

❀

fleeting daily mirages of hope
slipping through grips of butter fingers of reality
i walk the tired shores
dishevelled by the restless waves
to rescue my loitering mind

❀

amid growing wilderness
there will always be a sun
and you
saving me
from my yesterdays

❀

an angry sun and
a wrinkled soil in pain
down flow the tears
of clouds as rain
answered prayers

❀

a spell
of setting Sun
paused momentarily
steps of
approaching night

❀

a cloud burst
and the rains
wash away the dust
sheltering the mountain
like a perennial worry

❀

on the sands of time
a sea of hopes
beacons
i walk to meet
an unknown horizon

❀

waves
come running
like an
old friend
to hug me

❀

day in
and day out
the sea makes
the homely shells
into homeless dross

❀

a tree wiping
a tired face of setting Sun
before an enigmatic night
begins to write
nightmares

❀

a restless me
i try reaching for the moon
playing with waves
while it slips away
i'm left wet

❀

restless waves
return to catch
the Moon
sliced & splintered
in ecstatic love

❀

as the night folds
and dreams sublimate
the day breaks
with whiffs of timber
filling the with hope

❀

a few shadows
of yesterday
still bob
up and down
the silent coast

❀

when the day ends
but my voyage does not
i'll wait for dawn
of a golden morn
on an unknown kindly shore

❀

many windy kisses
and huge sunny assurances
cant keep the sea
on a full moon night
within its own confines

❀

shimmering summer sky
along the Horizon
she appears
full of soft notes
humming country songs

❀

an autumn bared trees
wearing a foggy attire
on the dock i recall
moments that refuse to fade
spent with you

❀

on the pavement
detached leaves
gather daily
to celebrate freedom
and the last flight

❀

in the creek
where reflections are meek
a single pebble
doesn't let their
images sleek

❀

converse
with universe
in solitude
answers appear slowly
from nothing

❀

a happy morn
soaked with the night's dreams
waltz of the wind
into another unsuspecting sunset
we walk together

❀

the secrets
walk in shadows
in the sky
openly
wanders the moon

❀

amidst the
striped reflections
the only sound
that resonated about
was of tranquility

❀

a nightfall letting
the shadows slip in safely
while i wait
for you to feel
the body & soul

on the sands of time
i walk in trance
imagining a door ajar
a welcome smile
and a final resting place